More
Funny Things
on the Way to Church

More

Funny Things

on the Way to Church

Compiled by Dave Anderson
Edited by Tim Wilcox

Illustrations by Lance Bowen

Publishing House
St. Louis

Copyright © 1983 Concordia Publishing House
3558 S. Jefferson Avenue, St. Louis, MO 63118

Manufactured in the United States of America

Library of Congress Cataloging in Publication Data
Main entry under title:

More funny things on the way to church.

     Continues: A Funny thing happened on the way to church.
     1. Christian life—Anecdotes, facetiae, satire, etc.
I. Anderson, Dave, 1943-   II. Wilcox, Tim. 1949-
BV4517.M67 1983   248.4'0207   82-23668
ISBN 0-570-03893-6 (pbk.)

---

2 3 4 5 6 7 8 9 10 WP 92 91 90

Preface

Stories from the first book, A FUNNY THING HAPPENED ON THE WAY TO CHURCH, have made their way to audiences across the United States, Scandinavia, Australia, Papua New Guinea, and a few other countries, evoking the "other" international language, laughter. Sometimes smiles, lots of giggles, and often tears from too much funny.

These stories have prompted pastors to provide a second collection of true anecdotes from their ministry—and now we have MORE FUNNY THINGS ON THE WAY TO CHURCH. Thanks to all who have contributed to this book—especially to Dr. Ted Matson for the material borrowed from his collection (now out-of-print) from the former Augustana Lutheran Church.

Doctors and psychologists tell us that it is *healthy* to laugh—we *need* it. These pages will help meet that need.

Seriously, you may really need to laugh and smile right now. Let us help you out.

Smile—mostly because God loves you!

Dave Anderson

Worshipers, Beware!

When my sister and her husband returned from mission service in Nigeria, Africa, they came to my rural parish for a visit.

One of their sons apparently wasn't familiar with a common sight in our part of the country—church cemeteries. When he saw all the gravestones outside the sanctuary, he turned to me with a puzzled look and said, "Uncle Robert, did all those people die in church?"

—The Rev. Robert Kruger
Carver, Minn.

Dust Off the Shotgun

Soon after I began my ministry in Dodge City, Kans., a couple asked me to marry them. He was 87; she, 84.

Despite their years and hard-won wisdom, we agreed that marriage counseling would be a good idea. One of the first questions I asked was, "Albert, why do you want to marry this woman?"

With a twinkle in his eye, the prospective groom replied, "It's not so much 'want to,' Pastor, as 'have to.'"

—The Rev. Harvey Hanneman
Dodge City, Kans.

Backyard Baptism?

Everyone except the baby smiled on cue: family members, sponsors, pastor. We were gathered around the font right after the baptismal service, waiting for the baby's 8-year-old brother to snap a Polaroid.

When the picture popped out, he grabbed it and exclaimed, "Oh, shoot! I didn't get the birdbath in."

—The Rev. F. E. Geske
Minneapolis, Minn.

A Tall, Skinny Kid

It must have been my handwriting. When I asked our new church secretary to put a birth announcement in Sunday's bulletin, this is what she typed and what the congregation read: "Born to the Smith family on March 3, a baby girl, 22 oz., 9 feet 3 inches long."

—The Rev. Harvey Hanneman
Dodge City, Kans.

A Devil of a Time

I'd never seen a prouder father in my life. In fact, everyone in the baptismal party was positively beaming. Behind us, friends and relatives watched and listened carefully. So I decided to give the best performance I could.

I did—until the part where the pastor asks, "Do you renounce the devil and all his works...?" Instead of the devil, I blooped out the family's name (let's use Smith here). What I said, then, was "Do you renounce the Smith, and all his works ...?"

That simply wasn't right, so I tried again: "Do you renounce the Smith and all his works...?" Mercy! I was stuck in a rut, so I moved on to the next part.

After the service, I was relieved when no one said a thing about my mixing up the Smiths and the devil. But a few weeks later, they asked for a letter of transfer to another congregation.

Can't say I blame 'em.

—The Rev. F. E. Geske
Minneapolis, Minn.

License to Prey

When a pastor friend approached my wife and me in the church parking lot, we thought he had come to admire our car. Instead he pointed at the license plate, which bore AMEN, and asked about its theological implications.

"Theological nothing!" replied my wife. "That's *my* car, and the plate reads, 'Ah, men!'"

—The Rev. Harvey Hanneman
Dodge City, Kans.

Lure of the Gospel

It was time for the children's sermon. So I called the kids forward to the altar steps and told them a story about Jesus and His disciples.

Then I asked a perfectly natural question: "When Jesus called the disciples to be fishers of men, what bait did he tell them to use?"

One little boy leaned toward my microphone and confidently replied, "Women."

—The Rev. Harvey Hanneman
Dodge City, Kans.

Eyes Closed, But . . .

Our 4-year-old grandson was the ringbearer at his uncle's wedding. Soon after beginning the service, the pastor said, "Let us pray." Holding the pillow with the wedding rings, our grandson exclaimed in a loud whisper, "But I can't fold my hands!"

—Mary Reed
Bethesda, Md.

Me too, Mom!

My wife, Erna, thought the day had come. She was wrong.

"The day" was to be our 3-year-old son's first time alone in the pew while his mother went forward for Communion. Erna thought, "He'll be OK."

But just as she received the bread, Nathan stood up and yelled, "I'm hungry too!"

There wasn't a straight face in church—two red ones, though. Guess whose.

—The Rev. Julius Kimpel
Stevensville, Md.

Blessed Nuisance

When August Martin Appleton was baptized in our congregation, the special service was printed separately and tucked in the bulletin. At one point, worshipers were surprised, then amused to read, "Through baptism God has made this new bother a member. . . ."

—Gene Rubley
Springfield, Ill.

LANCE BOWEN

Bedside Manners

Downright embarrassing. That's how I'd describe the day I visited a parishioner in the local hospital's intensive-care unit.

I was the intern pastor; the member, a heart attack patient who seemed to be recovering well. He, his wife, and I had an upbeat visit.

Before leaving, I stood with the wife to pray at her husband's bedside. By then I wasn't feeling well at all, since I'd just given blood. But that prayer was important. They expected it.

They didn't expect what happened soon after "Dear Lord." I fainted. When I came to, the poor woman was trying to lift me off her startled husband as she screeched for a nurse. (Picture it!)

Amazingly, the heart patient survived. My ego didn't.

—The Rev. Jack Harris
Princeton, Minn.

Cut the Chatter, Reverend!

On the first Friday of each month, I conduct a preaching service in the chapel of a nearby convalescent home. Since new faces appear every time, I like to begin by chatting informally for a few minutes.

Several months ago, I was doing just that when one woman interrupted, with a tinge of scolding in her voice: "When are you going to get started? I can't sit here forever!"

So much for small talk. On with the service.

—The Rev. Louis Nuechterlein
Cheshire, Conn.

Trackside Therapy

Both of us were frustrated. The Rev. Leonard Pankuch—a clergy colleague—and I sat together lamenting the extraordinary efforts it took to encourage creative programming in our parishes.

Len said it all with this: "At least once a month I go to the railway crossing to watch the trains. It's great to see something go through that I don't have to push!"

—The Rev. Jack Harris
Princeton, Minn.

My Word!

Among the biggest challenges for new missionaries is learning the language of the people they serve. Look-alike and sound-alike words can be confusing. They certainly were for my wife and me when we were struggling to master Malagasy, an African language.

One day, for instance, my wife told our baby-sitter in Malagasy to cook the baby. Then she told our cook to kill the bananas. Fortunately, our helpers had learned to understand "missionary talk." So the baby-sitter bathed the baby and the cook killed the chicken.

Another time, I told some Malagasy-speaking friends about my visit to the local jail. I meant to say something like "I visited prison this morning to preach to the people there." What I actually said, confusing similar words, was "I visited hell this morning to preach to the people there." Believe me, those friends of mine were surprised!

—The Rev. Carl Ulrich
Gaborone, Botswana

All Aboard, Please

The church convention in Fargo, N. Dak., brought delegates from all over. Some of them stayed at the FM Hotel in Moorhead, Minn., just across the river from Fargo.

Now, the hotel was near Moorhead's depot, and trains kept rolling in and out all night long. Early the next morning, a bleary-eyed delegate buzzed the hotel operator and asked, "When does this hotel arrive in Moorhead?"

—The Rev. Theodore Matson
Lake Geneva, Wis.

Coulda Kicked Myself

Hospital visitation has its ups and downs. Ask any pastor. Me, for instance.

While trying to encourage one of my members, I couldn't help hearing the moans and groans of another patient nearby. So after an uplifting chat with my parishioner, I stepped over to the poor woman's bed, determined to spread the cheer.

There I found a very large person lying flat on her back, the bed sheet pulled up to her chin. Reaching for one of her feet, outlined beneath the cover, I gave it a good shake. "Sure hope you're feeling better soon," I chirped. Her response was immediate and deafening— a ghastly shriek.

"Oh!" said my startled parishioner. "That's Mrs. Schwartz. She's just had foot surgery."

What could I do but apologize—and run for my car!

—The Rev. Jerry Straszheim
Coral Springs, Fla.

Priest's Privilege?

Just before visiting our new community hospital for the first time, I met with a Roman Catholic priest. We talked about supporting each other's ministry.

At the hospital I was pleased with the welcome accorded me as a minister. Especially impressive was a comfortable lounge marked "Father's Room." My Catholic colleague will be thrilled, I thought.

But what about Protestant clergy? Do they have a special room, too?

That's what I asked a passing nurse. She looked bewildered, then smiled, and finally just plain laughed.

Father's Room was in the maternity ward!

—The Rev. Jack Harris
Princeton, Minn.

Under the Influence?

While making calls at the local hospital, I visited with the parents of a boy who was having surgery. After talking of this and that over coffee, we went to his room—just as he was returning from post-op.

"Pastor's here," the mother said to her groggy son. He mumbled something in response, which made her chuckle.

I was curious and asked, "What did he say?"

"Well, Pastor," answered the mother, "he said, 'What disaster's here?'"

I dearly hoped he was still under the anesthesia's influence!

—The Rev. Edwin Rosenthal
Woodworth, N. Dak.

Such a Wine Fedding!

It was the young pastor's first wedding, and he was desperately determined to conduct the marriage without a hitch. Everyone could see he was nervous, but somehow he managed pretty well, for awhile.

Then came the words that, thankfully, have been removed from later service books—something like "Into this holy estate this man and woman come now to be united." Fine. But the follow-up came out, "If anyone, therefore, can show just cause why they may not be joyfully loined [instead of lawfully joined] together...."

Hearing no protests, the young pastor forged ahead to the ring ceremony, with growing confidence. But we in the pews pretty much lost ours when he said, "Now place the fing on her ringer."

—The Rev. David Issacson
Rocky Point, N.Y.

Pushin' Up Daisies

I should have made the connection sooner—a *lot* sooner.

The banner was right there in the front of the sanctuary, conspicuous as can be. Intended as a colorful exhortation to the congregation, it was hung a week or two before.

Before the funeral, that is. As I stood to begin the service, my eyes were opened. "Oh, Lord, no!" I groaned.

Looming large over the casket, the banner admonished, "Bloom where you are planted now."

—The Rev. Jack Harris
Princeton, Minn.

19

Lord, Have Mercy!

After all the others had risen from the Communion rail, I noticed one venerable member still on his knees, head bowed. "What humility!" I said to myself, admiring the man. Then he looked pleadingly my way. His tie was stuck in a joint of the rail.

—The Rev. John Damien
Tolna, S. Dak.

Praiseworthy Preachin'

While I was reveling in the buttering-up church-council members were giving me, one sweet woman reached the pinnacle of flattery with "Oh, we just love your sermons!" Wanting to hear more, I said, "Why's that?" "Because they're so short," she replied. I shouldn't have asked!

—The Rev. John Damien
Tolna, S. Dak.

Master Detectives

It was the last Sunday in Advent. For my children's talk I had the kids play Sherlock Holmes.

"There are clues all around us that Christmas is coming," I said. "Can you tell me a few?"

"All four candles are lit on the wreath," said one bright youngster.

"We have a special banner," said another.

"You're wearing blue ribbons [stoles]," observed a third.

21

Then came the clue that brought the house down. A boy whose family had not been attending worship regularly simply said, "We're here."

—The Rev. David Roschke
Houston, Tex.

Neither Are You

It's customary in many Roman Catholic parishes to exchange a formal greeting before the Gospel is read. "The Lord be with you," intones the priest. "And also with you," answers the congregation.

One Sunday the priest stepped up to the lectern, worried about a PA system that had failed him more than once. He fiddled with the switch, tapped the microphone, and adjusted the swivel. Finally he muttered in disgust, "This mike isn't working again." From the pews the answer boomed back: "And also with you."

—The Rev. Joseph Lorenz
Iberia, Mo.

Struttin' Their Stuff

The executive secretary of the Women's Missionary Society stepped proudly to the convention podium, financial report in hand. After detailing the past year's record of generous giving, she declared, "We ladies are really proud of our figures!"

—The Rev. Ken Engstrom
Miller, S. Dak.

Nice Polly

Grandpa tried again and again, but he never could find one particular parishioner at home. That puzzled him—until . . .

One day, as he was approaching the woman's house, he heard a voice through the front door, which was open for a change: "Run for your life! Here comes that blankety-blank preacher."

It was the parishioner's parrot—a well-trained bird indeed!

—Elizabeth Spitze
East Peoria, Ill.

Pray It Right!

She was Norwegian through and through—an old-country immigrant lying in a hospital bed far from the fjords.

Members of her large family, who tiptoed in and out of her room, knew the aging matriarch was near death. She had been silent for hours, eyes closed.

Her pastor got no response either. So he began the Lord's Prayer in Norwegian. Halfway through, he switched to German.

Suddenly, the woman's eyes flickered and opened. Then she fairly boomed in Norwegian: "What are you doing now? Can't you pray it right?" Just as suddenly, the gloomy atmosphere vanished.

To this day the family remembers, with chuckles, how Grandma was tricked by the pastor, even when she had decided to die.

—Ramona Cherland
North Battleford, Sask.

Bathroom Savvy

Congregational meetings can be tense and nerve-wracking at times, taxing the endurance of even the strongest members.

One year we decided to have coffee halfway through our meetings, since most of us needed a break. After a cup or two, a piece of coffee cake, and some socializing, I headed for the men's restroom.

There I said to a fellow member, "Things are really hot and heavy in the meeting." He agreed. "The only consolation," I continued, "is that even though they don't know what they're doing out there, we sure know what we're doing in here!"

—Paul Jorgensen
Eugene, Ore.

Little Devil's Debut

A youngster came home from his first Sunday school session. Right away his mother asked, "What did you learn today, Son?" "Oh," he said, "I learned about Jesus—and 'sit *down,* sit *down,* sit *down.*'"

—The Rev. R. G. Friedrichs
Houston, Tex.

She's a Goner!

It was a subzero day in January, but not too cold for a wedding. As I began the marriage meditation, I noticed that the bride was losing color fast. Cool and calm, I instructed her to kneel. That didn't help much.

So the photographer sent an usher forward with smelling salts, which revived the bride. Just to be safe, I had her sit in a chair after that.

On with the meditation. When I finished, I asked the congregation to turn to page 206 in *Lutheran Book of Worship* (I meant 203). Chuckles and then barely stifled laughter followed. "What!" I said to myself.

Only after the wedding did I discover my mistake. Page 206 in *LBW* begins the order for "Burial of the Dead."

—The Rev. Gary Panko
Grafton, Iowa

Oh, Really?

The pastor at a church read the Gospel and then absentmindedly blooped, "Here ends the kingdom of God."

—Mildred Tengbom
Anaheim, Calif.

Give Us a Break!

When my late friend, the Rev. August Waechter, was a pastor many years ago in Bunker Hill, Ill., it was not customary for clergy to have regular vacations.

Even so, he finally asked his congregation for permission to take one. The members agreed. Then he said, "Shall I arrange for a substitute pastor to conduct services while I'm gone?"

"Oh, no!" they chorused. "We want a vacation too!"

—The Rev. Eugene Smith
Los Angeles, Calif.

No, It Can't Be!

"You'll be preaching in three weeks," said my supervising pastor soon after I'd arrived to begin internship. I'd expected to be in the pulpit sooner but was grateful for the reprieve.

The big day approached and, as usual, I had everything organized. Part of my plan was to be at church for the 8 a.m. service by 6:45. That way I could practice a bit and get the feel of "the stage."

Horrors! I jerked awake at 7:40 a.m. and, eyes abulge, shook my wife. "Why didn't you wake me?" I fairly screamed.

She mumbled something, but I was already flying toward the bathroom, where I brushed my teeth for a few seconds. "Maybe I can shave after the first service," I said to myself. "But that hair. Oof! No time."

Time. Why hadn't the alarm gone off? Aha! It hadn't gone off because I'd never set it. I was racing around like a madman early *Saturday* morning.

Who me—anxious? Whatever gave you that idea?

—The Rev. Johnny Bell
Lordstown, Ohio

Onward, Christian Soldiers

Some time ago we phoned an orphanage in Brazil to ask how our congregation—Streams in the Desert Lutheran Church—could help. Maybe it was a missed translation or simply a bad connection. Whatever, the first letter we received from the orphanage was addressed to "Desert Firearms Lutheran Church."

—Charles Prokopp
Tucson, Ariz.

Woe Is Us!

I hadn't been in my first parish long when I began the after-service practice of joining with members in prayer at the altar.

One Sunday the bulletin announced: "TODAY, following worship—PRAYER AT THE ALTAR . . . for and with those who have special needs and concerns. Simply wail in the front pew."

—The Rev. John Anderson
Kelliher, Minn.

Generous to a Fault

Youngsters belonging to the Sunday school at Trinity Church in Rice Lake, Wis., were startled to read this bulletin announcement just before Christmas: "Any children bringing gifts for teachers this year will be given to the shut-ins."

—Christopher Miller
Rice Lake, Wis.

Precious Memories

In our mobile society, we often lose contact with old friends, who then remember us the way we were. Occasionally we see them again, by chance or choice— a good time to reminisce.

It was that way for my parents when they visited people in Arizona who had been our neighbors in Pennsylvania some 25 years before. The woman used to baby-sit my sister and me when we were still pre-schoolers, so she was anxious to hear all about us.

"Well," said my mother proudly, "Johnny's a pastor now."

Her pride deflated a moment later when the woman, memories intact, blurted, "What! That little devil!"

—The Rev. Johnny Bell
Lordstown, Ohio

Nasty Imposter

I had to be away from my parish one Sunday, so a guest pastor led worship. When he climbed into the pulpit, our 3-year-old son stared for a minute or so. Then he blurted: "He don't sound like my dad. That's *not* my dad. I'm goin' home!" And out he started.

—The Rev. Michael Haar
Lake City, Minn.

You OK, Lord?

I'm rarely ill, so when I had tonsillitis not long ago, it was the first time our 3-year-old son had seen me sick in bed. He apparently thought it was pretty serious and would check on me often to see how I was doing.

During one visit he stepped gravely to my bedside and said, "Dad, if you die, please don't give Jesus your sore throat."

I thought that concern was just wonderful. He wasn't worried about death or separation. He knew I'd be with Jesus and didn't want the Lord to catch my awful sore throat. (*P.S.* Don't worry about Jesus. I recovered.)

—The Rev. David Roschke
Houston, Tex.

ACRO-
PHOBIC

LANCE BOWEN

Ascension Day

My pastor came to see me just before I was wheeled into the hospital's operating room. At the end of his visit, he kneeled to pray—unaware that his knee was pressing against the bed-raising lever. After "Amen" he looked *up* at me, surprise covering his face. I simply smiled and said, "Thank you, Pastor, for that uplifting prayer."

—Alfred Buehner
Kettering, Ohio

Messy Minister

It happened when my father-in-law was a pastor in Woodward, Ill. While out visiting members, he stopped near noon at a farm. The farmer's wife, of course, invited him to stay for lunch.

Seated at the table, my father-in-law noticed he was the only one with a napkin. Half in jest he asked the farmer's wife, "How come I have a napkin but not your husband?"

"Oh," she replied quite seriously, "he doesn't slobber."

—The Rev. Eugene Smith
Los Angeles, Calif.

Words of Absolution

While preparing for Holy Communion with a dear, aging member who was almost deaf and blind, I read her the old prayer of confession: ". . . I have grievously

31

sinned against Thee in many ways, not only by outward transgressions, but also by secret thoughts and desires."

Right after the "Amen," she reached over, patted me on the knee, and said: "Don't worry, Pastor. I'm sure God will forgive you."

—The Rev. Robert Hereth
Chicago, Ill.

What a Relief!

Aunt Myrtle was a fiercely loyal Lutheran. When she was growing up, the worst thing that could happen was for a Lutheran to marry a Roman Catholic—a conviction that stuck with her into old age.

When one of her relatives brought home his fiancée, Aunt Myrtle took him aside to ask the big question: "What's her religion?"

"Well, um, uh, she's Buddhist," he almost whispered.

"Thank God!" cried Aunt Myrtle. "I was afraid she'd be Catholic."

—The Rev. Paul Frerking
Houston, Tex.

Dial-a-Prayer

While visiting members of the congregation I serve as director of Christian education, I was grateful for the privilege of joining them in family devotions. Their custom was to read the Bible and pray before dinner. So we did.

Then the mother, smiling broadly at her husband, said, "This reminds me of another time."

Seems the family had read Scripture, prayed, and was about to say grace when the phone rang. Up jumped the father, grabbed the phone, and said, "Come, Lord Jesus, be our guest . . ."

—James Haack
Carrollton, Mo.

My Blue Heaven

Our goldfish died after several years of carefree living in a bowl that was the centerpiece for a family-room table. The first time our baby-sitter came over after "the death," she immediately noticed the empty spot.

"Where's the fish?" she asked. Without hesitating, our 3-year-old shot back, "Oh, he's swimming with God."

—The Rev. David Roschke
Houston, Tex.

Herr Pastor's Harem

My wife and I had been feted by the congregation in honor of our wedding anniversary. One member, enjoying the celebration as much as we were, took me aside and enthusiastically shook my hand. "Pastor," he said, "I wish you many more of them—uh . . . anniversaries, I mean, not wives."

—The Rev. Ken Engstrom
Miller, S. Dak.

The Body of——Ouch!

It was the last thing I needed as a nervous intern.
Shuffling along the line of worshipers waiting for Holy
Communion, I placed a wafer in the mouth of each.
Suddenly an electric shock jumped from my fintertip to
the lips of one prayerful woman. Her head jerked back,
and I pulled my hand away in surprise. A moment later,
one wide-eyed communicant announced in a loud stage
whisper, "She *bit* him."

—The Rev. Carl Ulrich
Gaborone, Botswana

A Good Idea

Dr. Henry J. Hokenson, known to many as "Hokie,"
was a mission-board leader for years. Scheduled to give
a lengthy report at one annual meeting, Hokie led off
with "Before I talk, I want to say something."

—The Rev. Theodore Matson
Lake Geneva, Wis.

Smoke in the Grass

Back when P. O. Bersell was president of old
Augustana, he stopped by the church's seminary to
visit Dr. Conrad Bergendoff, the school's president.

Now Bersell was an avid cigar man, but he had
decided not to smoke as he walked with Bergendoff.
Midway across campus, Bersell spotted a good-sized
cigar butt lying in the grass. Pointing it out to his

companion, he said in jest, "Is that yours?"

Bergendoff paused for an instant, then deadpanned back: "No, go ahead. You saw it first."

—The Rev. Theodore Matson
Lake Geneva, Wis.

Altar Boy's Antics

I'll never forget that Sunday. Soon after the children's sermon, my wife stepped out of her pew and came forward. We met in the sacristy.

"Where's Christopher?" She asked. Christopher, our 3-year-old, had been with the kids up front while I spoke. But he hadn't returned with them.

"Oh, he'll turn up," I said, feigning confidence. "You'd better go sit down for the moment."

She headed back, only to be stopped by a member who whispered something in her ear and pointed at the chancel.

Back my wife came to the sacristy. "He's in the altar," she said. I couldn't believe it!

Sure enough, though—there was Christopher inside the free-standing altar, playing peekaboo with the congregation.

Instead of shouting, I motioned him out with forceful gestures. Then I wondered, "What do you do with your son, however naughty he's been, just after you've told the kids about Jesus scolding His disciples for stopping the little children from coming to Him?"

Well, I simply gave Christopher a big hug and sent him back to his mother. What would you have done?

—The Rev. Michael Haar
Lake City, Minn.

And for the Dummies . . .

It was time for a change—from Swedish to English. The church council voted in favor of starting with one English service a month. The pastor vehemently opposed it but bowed to the majority.

Not without getting in the last word, though. The Sunday before the big change, he made this announcement—In Swedish, of course: *"Nästa söndag skall vi ha svensk högmassa som vanligt. Söndag afton haller vi en engelsk gudstjänst för de mindre vetande."*

Translation: "Next Sunday morning we will have worship in Swedish as usual. In the evening there will be an English service for the less intelligent."

—The Rev. Theodore Matson
Lake Geneva, Wis.

Music Hath Charms

Our Sunday school Christmas pageant is an annual extravaganza—lots of kids, lots of teachers, lots of family and friends.

At the end of the 1981 program, all 200 children were marched up front for the grand finale. Seconds into the big number, a first-grader accidentally bumped his second-grade brother. The older boy promptly pushed back, knocking his brother into another youngster, who fell against another, and so on—almost like dominoes. Soon about 15 children in the front rows were pushing and punching one another.

Horrified, the choir director jumped into the middle of the melee. Then the pianist looked up, noticed the director was gone, and promptly lost her place in the music.

Staring disaster in the face, our quick-thinking director of Christian education jumped to her feet in the front pew and loudly let the little angels through the final verse of their song: "Let there be peace on earth, and let it begin with me."

—Eilene Harris
New Brighton, Minn.

Green Clean

A few people are questioning the wisdom of letting the men's group use the kitchen at Grace Church in Bellevue, Wash. Why? Not long ago a group member, who had been searching for detergent, was caught pouring lime Kool-Aid into the dishwasher.

—Olin Dasher
Edmonds, Wash.

Unetical Vatchdog

The elderly, very Swedish clergyman was determined to serve a particular church college with distinction. Elected to its board of directors, he made it his special concern to guard the school against the pagan influence of secular—particularly Greek—philosophy.

At one board meeting, he reacted strongly to a report calling for a new ethics course that would touch on the thinking of Greek philosophers. Fumed the pastor: "Etics! Etics! Vhat have vee to do vit etics? Dis iss a *Christian* institution!"

—The Rev. Theodore Matson
Lake Geneva, Wis.

Baby Boom Bomb

I became pastor of a certain congregation in 1945. Because many of "the boys" were just coming home from World War II, I soon was performing one wedding after another.

The following year, to no one's surprise, baptisms were the thing. One Sunday I had three. After the service, a faithful old woman grabbed my hand at the door and, in front of half the membership, loudly exclaimed: "Oh, Pastor, since you came we've had so many babies!"

—The Rev. Carl Schuette
Caney, Kans.

Telltale Teeth

The two sisters were members of his congregation in Chicago, so Pastor O. B. Hanson said their story is true.

Anyway, they had a widowed father, who, from time to time, would disappear in drink for a day or two. On one occasion, though, he was gone longer than that. So the sisters reported him missing.

A few hours later the police called to say a body had been found in the Chicago River. They suspected it was the missing father and asked the sisters to come and identify the waterlogged victim.

When the sisters entered the morgue, they saw the corpse—in bad shape—lying on a slab. It's mouth was open and its false teeth had dropped out of place.

"Oh," exclaimed one sister, "that's not father. He doesn't have false teeth."

40

As they were leaving, the undertaker walked over to the corpse and hissed: "You old fool! You could have had a fine Christian funeral if you'd only kept your mouth shut!"

—The Rev. Theodore Matson
Lake Geneva, Wis.

Let's not Mince Words

Years ago the old Augustana Lutheran Church voted in convention to make the change in the Apostle's Creed. For "descended into hell," they substituted "descended into Hades."

This caused no end of confusion, because some Augustana pastors and congregations refused to make the change. So, eventually, the original phrase was restored.

The Minneapolis *Tribune* took note of the action with a bold, front-page headline: "Augustana Lutheran Church Goes Back to Hell."

—The Rev. Theodore Matson
Lake Geneva, Wis.

Thanks a Lot, Son!

When Pastor Leonard Smith stepped into the pulpit of his Iowa church one Sunday, his 5-year-old son loudly announced, "Now comes the part I don't like."

—The Rev. Theodore Matson
Lake Geneva, Wis.

What's Big and Gray and Wears a White Collar?

For a few years in the 1950s, I was an interim pastor in Harriman, Tenn., some 20 miles from my home in Oak Ridge. Content with a fill-the-gap pastor for a while, members of the Harriman congregation hoped to have a full-time minister before 1960.

Anyway, an article appeared one day in the Harriman *Record* to explain my temporary status. It started out just fine, but somehow the newspaper substituted several lines (indicated here by *italics*) from a Baptist preacher's talk about, among other things, the domesticated elephants of India. Here's how part of the article went:

"Presently a resident pastor is being sought, but until one arrives, the Rev. J. V. Kimpel will *object. When they draw near, he pulls the harder, bending low his head and lifting his tail, and takes the bit into his teeth, pulling shamelessly.*"

Members of the congregation had a lot of fun with that—and with me. A typical comment from non-members: "We're sure comin' to your church to see what that preacher looks like!"

Was I upset? Not at all. The article did the parish more good than a thousand dollars worth of advertising.

—The Rev. Julius Kimpel
Stevensville, Md.

X-Rated Event

The annual Passion Sunday breakfast is a men's-club tradition at St. Paul Church in Chicago. Last year some of the newer members of St. Paul must have been puzzled by the breakfast announcement. Its closing line: "This is an adults-only affair."

—Doris Nordstrom
Addison, Ill.

Tempting Typo

Some members joked afterward that worship that morning had been specially organized by the single-adults group. Anyway, when we sat down for the matins service, few of us missed the bold heading in the bulletin: "ORDER OF MATING."

—The Rev. Bob Grosch
Oakland, Calif.

For the Winter Weary: Timely Advice

Late March, and two feet of snow still covered the ground. Then the weatherman predicted another blizzard. Even for a Minnesota winter, that was overdoing it!

So I asked the church custodian to put this message on our outdoor signboard: "Spring is coming. But, Lord, how long?"

A few days later the answer appeared on the signboard of the church directly across the street: "Be patient, my son, for with the Lord one day is as a thousand years."

—The Rev. Jack Harris
Princeton, Minn.

Don't You Dare!

She simply didn't want to go. That was clear to me and to other involuntary evesdroppers at the Memphis airport.

A man, who turned out to be her son, had just purchased a plane ticket for his elderly mother. The family was there to see her off, but, hearing the roar of jet engines, she turned stubborn.

I listened to the back-and-forth "conversation" for a few minutes, then, when I realized the family was Christian, introduced myself as a pastor.

"I'm going on the same flight," I said to the grandmother. "Will you sit with me?" To everyone's surprise and relief, she consented.

All went well aboard the plane—until it left the ground. My new friend became tense, then seemed about to panic. I thought, Better say something quick. So I tried "Have you asked for God's protection?"

"No, I haven't, young man," she said. "And don't you pray for me either. I don't want God to know I'm up here."

—The Rev. Eldon Weisheit
Tucson, Ariz.

I'm Not Amused

On Communion Sundays, it's the custom in one congregation I serve for children to come forward with their parents to be blessed. As I distributed the bread to a young couple one morning, their vocal 2-year-old announced, "Daddy's sandwich." Everyone at the rail smiled.

Then I came around with the wine. The child had been shushed before but spoke up once more: "Daddy's beer." Everyone smiled again—except Daddy.

—The Rev. Dave Eitland
Mountain, N. Dak.

So Why Should I?

A farmer down South had just harvested another fine cotton crop. When he told his pastor about the top price he expected to get for the bales, the pastor said, "You'll have enough, then, to pay your debts, and you can give a little extra to the church."

"Maybe I won't be givin' extra," said the farmer, "and I'll tell you why. If'n I don't pay the doctor, he don't come no more. And if'n I don't pay the grocer, he don't let me have no food. But if'n I don't pay the preacher, I just can't tell no difference at all."

—The Rev. Alvin Walter
Hillsboro, Tex.

That Bad, Was It?

When it's annual meeting time at our church, the women all bring something tasty for a fellowship meal prior to the business. Thanks to a typographical error in the local paper one year, some folks may have thought we enjoyed the food but not what followed.

The report: "At the church's annual meeting, a potluck dinner was served after which the business meeting was hell."

—John Florea
Aurora, Nebr.

Hooray!

My first parish was in Plains and Thompson Falls, Mont. After seven years with those fine people, I decided to take another call.

How could I tell them? And when? The Sunday right after I'd accepted the call seemed too soon. "I'll wait awhile," I said to myself. But just before the closing hymn of the service, I realized I'd have to break the news then. So I did.

A moment later, as the organ swelled, I marched out while my beloved parishioners sang, "On our way rejoicing."

—The Rev. Michael Boye
Conrad, Mont.

The Bible Tells Me So

After worship at Gloria Dei one morning, four of us decided to go for a Sunday drive. My three passengers were pillars of the church, all women in their 80s.

As we rolled through the countryside, our conversation turned to "the last days" and how earthquakes will increase before the end.

"We won't need to worry about that," said one of the women. "The earthquakes will all be at the bottom of the sea."

"They will?" I said, barely disguising my skepticism.

"Oh, yes!" she answered confidently. "The Bible says the earthquakes will be in 'diver's places.'"

—Lillian Thompson
Cupertino, Calif.

Junior High Hit Squad

I thought it was a straightforward test question for my confirmation students: "Can a pastor be fired? If not, how can he or she be removed?"

I got a variety of answers. One in particular shook me up a bit: "Pastors cannot be fired, but they can be terminated by death."

—The Rev. Ronald Kreiensieck
Fontana, Calif.

Cluck, Cluck, Cluck

It was an Easter custom at Bethany Church in Lindsborg, Kans. Women from surrounding farms would bring eggs and place them on the altar.

One year, right after the procession, Pastor Alfred Bergin stood up and boomed: "Thank you, ladies, for the eggs you've laid on the altar."

—The Rev. Theodore Matson
Lake Geneva, Wis.

Cure for Baldness

It's a special time in worship when children of the congregation come forward to watch a Baptism. Knowing that members of the preschool class had been studying the Sacrament, I asked them one morning at the font, "Why do we use water in Baptisms?" A thoughtful youngster piped up immediately, "To make the baby's hair grow." Hmmm.

—The Rev. James Boler
Webster Groves, Mo.

Strange Bedfellow

He was a devout and simple soul who desperately wanted to be elected to some church position. But that honor was denied him year after year. Finally, though, he was chosen to serve as an alternate delegate to the annual district convention.

That pleased him immensely, and he rushed home to tell his wife. But she was asleep.

As soon as she awoke the next morning, though, the dam of enthusiasm broke. "Lena, know what?" he almost shouted. "You've been sleeping with a substitute all night!"

—The Rev. Theodore Matson
Lake Geneva, Wis.

How Shall I Put It?

Small talk before worship—that's all it was. The visiting American pastor asked his Nigerian counterpart "Are you married?"

The African pastor, who knew bits and pieces of English, answered, "Yes, I have taken a wife."

Then the American asked, "Do you have any children?"

"No," said the Nigerian, "my wife is inconceivable." Noting the American's puzzled look, he tried, "I mean, she is impregnable."

Now the American pastor struggled in vain to suppress a smile.

"You see," revised the African pastor, "she is unbearable."

—The Rev. Harold Hein
Fort Worth, Tex.

Identity Crisis

Back when I was pastor of a big-city congregation, I always had members to visit in the hospital.

One day—Thanksgiving, in fact—I was a patient myself. The doctor had told me I needed minor surgery.

Before I checked in, though, I stopped to visit a sick parishioner. When she heard I would soon be on the operating table, she was concerned—and a bit confused, too. "Pastor," she said warmly, "I'm so sorry you have to have a hysterectomy." I never cracked a smile.

But a few minutes later, I had to laugh. Someone, a woman, was in my room. So I stopped a passing nurse and showed her my room card.

"Oh," she said, "I think you're in room 320-B."

I looked at the card. It read "32-OB" and, sure enough, I was standing right in the middle of the obstetrics ward!

—The Rev. Carl Schuette
Caney, Kans.

She Really Should

In our Sunday school program, we present certificates for memorization of the Lord's Prayer, the Apostles' Creed, and the Ten Commandments.

One 4-year-old boy was encouraged by his mother to learn the Lord's Prayer. "You'll get something special if you say it to the Sunday school director," she told him.

To which he promptly replied: "Why? Doesn't she know it?"

—Eilene Harris
New Brighton, Minn.

... To Us Be Blessed——Yuch!

A clergy colleague of mine stopped for lunch in a country cafe. After the food had been served, he bowed his head in prayer. The waitress, apparently watching her customer, bustled over with a look of concern on her face. "What's the matter, mister?" she asked. "Is there a worm in your salad?"

—The Rev. Ken Engstrom
Miller, S. Dak.

Must Be a Prophet

Preachers may deny it, but most are disappointed if no one compliments them at the door after worship.

A pastor I knew probably got quite a few after-service boosts in his time. This may have been his favorite: "Every one of your sermons is better than the next!"

—The Rev. Theodore Matson
Lake Geneva, Wis.

Now, that's Livin'!

The pastor stopped by to see one of his most active members on her 95th birthday. At the end of their visit, he said, "Well, I hope I'l be able to help you celebrate your 100th birthday."

With a twinkle in her eye, she looked him over and said: "You seem healthy enough, Pastor. I think you'll make it!"

—The Rev. George Steinbeck
Paso Robles, Calif.

Firstfruits?

I had just finished my talk to a church-women's group in St. Paul, Minn. After the benediction, everyone stood to leave.

All of a sudden, the group's president cried out: "Vait a minute! Don't forget that vee are to bring vith us yunk for Yesus next month."

—The Rev. Theodore Matson
Lake Geneva, Wis.

Mystery Guest

It was a hard act to follow. The secretary of the Young Women's Missionary Society had been invited by a Midwest congregation to speak to its mission group. The woman in charge stepped up to the microphone, looked at the esteemed visitor hesitantly, then proceeded with this introduction:

"We have a guest with us today who will speak to us. I believe she is from Chicago, or maybe it's Minneapolis. I'm not certain of her name or just why she is here, but we welcome her and call on her at this time."

—The Rev. Theodore Matson
Lake Geneva, Wis.

Enough Already!

After church one Sunday, I decided to go directly to the local nursing home to visit a parishioner. When I arrived it seemed all the wheelchair patients were lined up in the corridor for lunch.

As I made my way to the parishioner's room, still in my clericals, I stopped now and then to touch an outstretched hand and say a comforting word. Then I came to a tiny woman who looked at me quizzically, threw up her hands, and moaned: "Good God! Who are they bringing in here now?"

—The Rev. J. J. Vajda
St. Louis, Mo.

No Need to Be Chicken

Almost everybody in that small rural village belonged to the Lutheran congregation. One man, a bachelor, was not a member. But he attended worship regularly.

Finally, the pastor visited him and said: "Listen, Anders, it's good to see you every Sunday, but why don't you take your place as a member of the congregation?"

Anders replied: "That I cannot do, Pastor. You see, I was converted at a revival meeting. I could not therefore become a Lutheran."

To which the pastor responded: "What does that have to do with your church membership? Peter was converted by a rooster. That didn't mean he had to live in a chicken coop!"

—The Rev. Theodore Matson
Lake Geneva, Wis.

Let Me Explain, Explain

When a member of a small Wisconsin congregation visited Minneapolis some years ago, he worshiped in a "big city" church for the first time.

Upon returning to the rural parish, he was asked if anything about the service was different. "Yes," he replied, "they sing anthems."

The next question, of course, was "What's an anthem?"

The traveler thought for a moment, then said: "Well, anthems are like hymns, but different. If I was to sing, 'The cow is in the pasture,' that would be a hymn. But if I sang, 'The cow, the cow, is in the pasture, the pasture, the pasture,' *that* would be an anthem."

—The Rev. Theodore Matson
Lake Geneva, Wis.

The Magic Word

In a certain rural congregation it was the custom for members to stand after the sermon, when the pastor said, "Amen." One Sunday the sermon was based on the Epistle lesson. About five minutes into his homily, the pastor read a portion of the text. It was one of Paul's well-known doxologies, which end in amen. Sure enough, the congregation immediately stood up, and, to the pastor's surprise, his sermon was over.

—The Rev. Ray Tiemann
Cameron, Tex.

Declare Ye, Now

The calls went out one after the other. John Melvin accepted and became assistant pastor of Calvary Church. But Phillip Johnson, called to be pastor, needed more time to think.

After 30 days, the time allotted to consider a call, no answer had come. So Pastor Melvin sent Pastor Johnson a telegram that simply said, "Matthew 11:3."

An appropriate verse, indeed: "Are you he who is to come, or shall we look for another?"

—The Rev. Theodore Matson
Lake Geneva, Wis.

Right Gift, Wrong Giftee

A proud mother planned to give her son a Bible for confirmation and phoned her order to the publishing house to speed delivery.

She gave her name and address to the clerk at the other end, stipulated the number of the Bible from the catalog, and asked for the deluxe, red buckram binding.

To her relief the package arrived the day before Palm Sunday. But her jaw dropped when she opened the box and saw the name in bright gold lettering: RED BUCKRAM.

—The Rev. J. J. Vajda
St. Louis, Mo.

Caveat Pastor

The font was full for Baptism. As Dr. Karl Olander—then pastor of Trinity Church in Worchester, Mass.—dipped into the water, the baby's 6-year-old brother leaped up in the front pew. "Be careful!" he said anxiously. "She bites!"

—The Rev. Theodore Matson
Lake Geneva, Wis.

The Gospel Quartet

Full understanding of God is impossible for human beings. A bedtime discussion between my two sons and me illustrates this truth.

"There are lots of gods, aren't there?" asked 5-year-old Jeff.

I said no and added something about God being everywhere, all around us.

But Jeff still insisted on "lots of gods," naming the Father, Son, and Holy Spirit.

Before I could launch into an easy-to-understand explanation of the Trinity, 3-year-old Jason piped up from under his covers, "And then there's Godzilla."

—Roberta Bodensteiner
Cedar Falls, Iowa

What Did He Say?

At the time many immigrant churches were slowly switching to English, a pastor who knew little of the language was asked to conduct a military funeral service. He was determined to get along in the "new tongue," so the night before he spent several hours with English aids.

Next day the solemn occasion—complete with bugle corps—went smoothly until its conclusion. Then the pastor, by that time feeling confident and not a little proud, made this announcement: "Now, while the corps [pronounced as it's spelled] plays music, we'll all pass around the beer [bier], and we'll let those in union suits pass out first."

—Mavis Rogness
Toronto, S. Dak.

Cloning Clergy Clothes

Once a year at Christmas, when the kids line up for our church's traditional children's processional, I "huddle" with them in a Sunday school room to bring encouragement and chase away butterflies. As always, they come dressed in their finest clothes—usually new, since most have outgrown the previous year's outfits.

The children were all scrubbed and polished for Christmas '81. When I stepped into the room, fully robed, one little boy rushed up to show me his new clothes. Then, in total dismay, he looked me over and said, "But, Pastor, you wore that same outfit last year!"

—The Rev. A. R. Gallert
Beloit, Wis.

They What!

Members of a rural congregation in Kansas were gathered to raise money for a new sanctuary carpet. Slips of paper had been distributed for pledging—but apparently not to everyone.

From the balcony came this impromptu announcement: "Mrs. Johnson and I want to do something on the carpet, but we don't have any paper."

—The Rev. Theodore Matson
Lake Geneva, Wis.

All Scripture Is Inspired

I was pleased when a certain couple asked me to marry them. In the course of our conversation, I inquired where they would live after the wedding.

Oakland, Calif., they told me.

Then I said, "May I write to the pastor of St. Paul's Church there and ask him to call on you?" They replied, "Please, do."

Three weeks later, Pastor Lloyd Burke of St. Paul's sent me this note: "Dear Padre—Luke 14:22. Yours obediently, Lloyd."

I immediately turned to Luke 14:22 and read, "Sir, what you commanded has been done, and still there is room."

—The Rev. Theodore Matson
Lake Geneva, Wis.

David's Demise

Sunday school teachers often wonder if they're getting the lessons across to their students. Incidents like the following one are not encouraging.

A family was sitting around talking about a friend whose name was David. The parents explained to their 5-year-old son that he really didn't know David, because he'd never met him.

"Oh, yes! I know him," protested the youngster. "David was a king, but he got killed by the Salvation Army."

—Eilene Harris
New Brighton, Minn.

Hush, Now, Ye Loudmouth

Before being ordained, I used to lead the singing Sunday morning at my home church. Once, before the service began, I had to teach the congregation a new hymn.

A woman who had emotional difficulties came in late for rehearsal. Soon after sitting down in one of the back pews, she jumped to her feet and shouted: "Would you mind letting *me* know what hymn you're singing? I'd like to sing it too!"

I answered immediately, unaware how appropriate my response would be: "Let all mortal flesh keep silence."

—The Rev. Steve Binsfeld
Waite Park, Minn.

Passin' the Buck to Pastor

I was reasonably relaxed before a funeral, chatting with mourners in what we call our worship court.

Then a man I didn't know (let's call him Mr. A) approached me. "Pastor, do you know that gentleman over there?" he asked, pointing to a man we'll call Mr. B.

"No, I don't think I do," I replied.

"Well," said Mr. A, "his fly is open."

Good grief! What was I supposed to do?

But before I could say, "Let it be," Mr. A asked, "Don't you think he should be told?"

"Yes, yes, of course," I answered impatiently. When Mr. A walked over to Mr B, I smiled at life's minor pitfalls and felt certain the matter soon would be closed.

But a moment later, to my chagrin and dismay, Mr B tapped me on the shoulder. "Pastor," he said, "that man over there says you have something to tell me."

—The Rev. Eldon Weisheit
Tucson, Ariz.

Bad Enough, Buster!

In the old days when Iowa and Nebraska were "gettin' out of the mud"—grading roads in preparation for pavement—Rev. J. Victor Carlson was traveling about for Immanuel Deaconess Institute of Omaha.

Coming home after one trip, Pastor Carlson let his concentration slip into neutral for a moment. Off the road he went. Perched precariously on the soft shoulder, his car was in danger of toppling over.

A couple of local farmers came to the rescue. "Look out or you'll go to hell!" one shouted to the clergyman, who sat in the Ford scarcely daring to move.

"No, sir," said Carlson calmly. "I'm goin' to Omaha. But that's bad enough!"

—The Rev. Theodore Matson
Lake Geneva, Wis.

He's a Brute, Pastor

"It's hopeless," she told me, and I could see she was about to cry.

Their marriage was on the rocks. The wife talked about her husband's hostility, about his volcanic temper, and about how he was always accusing her of nagging him.

"Let's suppose for a moment that you never nag your husband," I suggested. "Why does he *think* you do?"

That puzzled her, and she paused to think. Just as I was about to break the silence, she sighed and said, "Because I nag him all the time."

—The Rev. Jerome Teichmiller
Clifton, Tex.

Oinks a Lot!

The doorbell rang. It was a parishioner, and my clergy friend said, "Come on in." The member didn't have time, but she did have an armful of bottles, which she handed him with these words: "Pastor, since we don't have pigs anymore, we thought you should have this milk."

—The Rev. A. A. Hanson
Clarissa, Minn.

How About "Marvin"?

My grandfather, the Rev. J. F. Lorch, told me about a Baptism he performed one Sunday. The service went just fine until he asked for the baby's name.

"The baby's name?" chorused the parents, exchanging puzzled glances. "Why, *you* name the baby when you baptize it."

—Elizabeth Spitze
East Peoria, Ill.

Now What, Mom?

When my grandfather called on a woman who had stopped coming to church, he found her daughter sitting on the porch.

"I'm the pastor," he said. "Is your mother at home?"

"Oh, uh . . . no," answered the youngster. "She's gone."

So Grandpa sat down to ask the daughter some

questions. After a while, though, she got fidgety and finally stood up.

"Excuse me," the little girl said, and she walked over to the front door. Then, bending to the keyhole, she whispered loudly: "Mama, I've told him all you told me to, and he's still here. Now what should I tell him?"

—Elizabeth Spitze
East Peoria, Ill.

Dyin' to Get In

"What are we going to do about the fence?" It was the same old question, asked at every annual meeting of the New England congregation by the same old member. He wanted a fence around the church cemetery.

Finally one year, the pastor lost patience. Isolating the "fencer" with a steely stare, he said, "Is there anyone in the cemetery who wants to get out?" "No," replied the member. "Is there anyone outside who wants to get in?" the pastor asked. "No," again.

"Then," concluded the pastor, "forget the fence!"
He did.

—The Rev. Theodore Matson
Lake Geneva, Wis.

Not a Good Sign

A middle-aged Swedish couple asked the local pastor to marry them. "When and what time?" he asked.

They named a date but couldn't agree on a time.

She wanted 11 a.m. He pushed for a late-afternoon or evening wedding. So they argued back and forth.

Growing impatient, the pastor interrupted and asked the groom-to-be why he opposed an early wedding. "Vell," he replied, "if vee get married in the morning, vhat are vee going to doo all day?"

—The Rev. Theodore Matson
Lake Geneva, Wis.

Preacher's Pun-ishment

If a contest were held for creative sermon titles, I could pull one from my memory that surely would be among the winners.

When I was growing up near Joplin, Mo., one of my father's closest friends was a fellow pastor. Well, the two of them drove by the local Baptist church one day and did a double doubletake at the sign out front. The Sunday evening sermon, it announced, would be "Giving the Pigs a Permanent Wave."

Neither pastor could imagine what the preacher's text would be, so my father's friend volunteered to attend the service.

Monday morning he called Dad to clear up the mystery. The sermon, he reported, was about the prodigal son. Toward the end of his own version of that great parable, the Baptist preacher had intoned, "The prodigal, while feeding the swine, thought about how well his father's slaves were treated. Then he came to his senses and gave the pigs a permanent wave."

—The Rev. Paul Frerking
Houston, Tex.

Nice of Him to Call

Each Easter, Church of Christ the Redeemer in Minneapolis would order hot-crossed buns from the local baker. One year, right after the high holy day, the womens-group president called the bakery to express appreciation.

The employee who answered cupped the phone for a moment and shouted to the baker: "It's Christ the Redeemer calling to thank you for the excellent buns."

To which the baker replied, "Tell Him I'm glad He enjoyed them."

—Al Girtz
Salina, Kans.

Great Expectations

Grandpa was a pastor for years—no, make that decades. One of his strangest encounters in all that time was with a newly married—and quite naive—couple.

Seems they called him over to their house one afternoon, along with the local doctor and a nurse. The five of them sat around for an hour or so, making small talk. Finally Grandpa's curiosity got the best of him. "Say, what are we doin' here anyway?" he asked.

"Well," said the young husband, smiling at his wife, "we've been married nine months today."

Soon after that, the three visitors left. Two and a half years later, the couple finally had a baby.

—Elizabeth Spitze
East Peoria, Ill.

It'll Have to Do

Our church has a program to collect food for needy people. We call it "Green Tape."

Twice a year the Sunday school children receive a paper lunch bag along with a note that explains the program. The following week they are supposed to return the bags with canned goods in them.

Well, on one of those return Sundays a 4-year-old presented his brown-bag offering with some trepidation. "We didn't have any green tape," he sighed, "so my mom put some food in here instead."

—Eilene Harris
New Brighton, Minn.

Inflated Luck

It was church cleanup day, and a 5-year-old had volunteered to help with my assignment.

On our rounds, we found a penny under a pew. "Pick it up and put it in your shoe," I said to my assistant. "It'll bring you luck."

Then I felt guilty. "It's not really lucky," I told the child.

"I know," she said. "But if I found $300, *that* would be lucky!"

—Susan Ruth
Baldwin Park, Calif.